THOMAS & FRIENDS

Nia's Balloon Bl

Based on a story by **Patrick Rieger**

Adapted by **Fiona Munro**

DEAN

First published in Great Britain 2024 by DEAN, part of Farshore
An imprint of HarperCollins*Publishers*
1 London Bridge Street, London SE1 9GF
www.farshore.co.uk

HarperCollins*Publishers*
Macken House, 39/40 Mayor Street Upper,
Dublin 1, D01 C9W8, Ireland

Based on a story by Patrick Rieger
Adapted by Fiona Munro

Based on the Railway Series by The Reverend W Awdry.

ISBN 978 0 00 870677 7
Printed in China
001

A CIP catalogue record for this title is available from the British Library.

It was a sunny day on the island of Sodor. Thomas and Kana were chugging past an exciting-looking billboard.

"I just LOVE parades!" said Kana.

They were admiring the floats and giant balloons on the poster when Nia came whizzing alongside. They watched as a train floated into the sky.

"***WHOAA!*** It's a flying train!" laughed Thomas.

"It's not a flying train," giggled Nia. "It's a train balloon that I get to hold in the parade later."

12

They heard a honk and turned to see Emily rolling along. Sir Topham Hatt was riding in her passenger car.

"Greetings everyone! You three look ready for the Vicarstown Parade."

"We are!" said Thomas.

"I'm bringing this balloon." said Nia.

"Wonderful!" said Sir Topham Hatt. Suddenly, a gust of wind blew his hat off his head. "Just be careful out there. It's a bit windy today."

"I hope the wind doesn't blow the balloon away before the parade!" said Thomas, sounding worried.

"I'll whizz it through the mountain pass, where high rock walls will block the wind," Nia began.

"Then I'll head through the forest, where the trees will keep the wind away, and lastly I'll zip through the Tunnel of Zoom, where the wind always stays outside."

"Come on," said Kana, beginning to move down the track. "We'd better head to the mountains before it gets windier!"

But there were jagged cliffs on both sides of the narrow mountain pass. They were worried the balloon might pop!

"I've got this!" said Thomas, as he wedged himself between the rocks and the balloon.

At last, Thomas, Kana, Nia and the balloon arrived safely on the other side of the mountain and into a forest of trees gently swaying in the breeze.

"That was tougher than I thought! But we're safe from the wind in here," said Nia.

18

"We may be safe from the wind," said Thomas, looking around at the crazily waving branches, "but what about the trees?"

The spiky branches began to sway back and forth around the balloon as Nia did her best to keep it out of their way.

"If only we could get the wind to blow away from us!" said Nia.

"Maybe we can!" said Thomas, who suddenly had a great idea. "Kana, I think it's time for a ***WHOOSH!***"

Kana smiled and began to roll slowly backward and then, a moment later, zoomed ahead.

WHOOSH!

As Kana's lightning speed forced the branches to bend away from them, Nia and Thomas rushed along the track, coming out on the other side of the forest just as the trees sprang back into place.

"Thanks, Kana," said Nia. "It's a good thing we're almost at ..."

"... the Tunnel of Zoom!"

As the friends got closer and closer to the tunnel entrance, they realised it looked too small. The balloon was not going to fit through.

"Hmm ... the balloon is bigger than I thought," said Nia.

18

Luckily, Thomas had another good idea.

"Nia, you go into the tunnel and we'll take care of the rest."

Nia didn't look so sure, but chugged slowly into the tunnel.

Thomas and Kana watched as the big balloon stopped Nia going any further.

"Just follow me," said Thomas to Kana as he charged at full speed toward the balloon.
"***PUSH!***"

At last, the balloon squeezed into the tunnel and then, a few seconds later … popped out on the other side, with Thomas and Kana rattling along close behind.

Just as the friends were catching their breath, a gust of wind tugged the balloon up and ***SNAP!*** went the string.

"The balloon! It's getting away!" shouted Nia.

"It's going toward Lookout Mountain," shouted Thomas. "We can grab it from above!"

"But how are we going to hook it back onto the string?" Nia puffed.

Kana thought quickly. "Sandy and Carly have hooks!" she said, speeding off. "I'll go and get them."

Thomas and Nia chugged on toward Lookout Mountain.

"Look!" said Thomas, seeing their friends waiting on the track high above.

"The balloon isn't going the right way! Let's try to blow it toward them."

They both puffed as hard as they could.

As they all watched, the balloon began to sail higher, gently floating closer and closer to the peak. Just as it was about to drift out of reach, Sandy reached out her claw to grab the string.

"Don't worry, I got it … I got it …" she said.

"C'mon!" said Thomas as he led the way up the winding track toward the others.

Suddenly, a powerful gust of wind lifted the balloon even higher and dragged poor Sandy toward the edge.

Carly gasped. "Hang on!" and rushed to grab Sandy with her crane hook. Now they were BOTH in danger of toppling over the edge of Lookout Mountain!

“Help!” they shouted as all the engines behind coupled up together and rushed forward to help. They pulled as hard as they could until everyone was safely back on the track.

“One balloon …” said Carly at last, “ready for the parade!”

The tired but happy friends arrived at the parade just in time. Sir Topham Hatt was there to greet them.

"Wonderful!" he declared. "Let the parade begin!"

"Hey... you all want to help me carry the balloon in the parade?" asked Nia.

"***ABSO-TOOT-LY!***" said Thomas with a smile.